SPECIAL NEW ZEALAND'S SOUTH ISLAND TRAVEL GUIDE 2023

Exploring the Natural Wonders of New Zealand

Nameem Rumberg

TABLE OF CONTENTS

INTRODUCTION

Welcome to the astounding, friendly, and engaging, Special New Zealand's south island travel guide for 2023! This guidebook is perfectly in line with world standards and packed with amazing information to help you make the most of your visit to the South Island.

This region of New Zealand is known for its incredible beauty and diverse range of activities and attractions. This detailed guide will take you through the special features of New Zealand's South Island, such as the stunning Fiordland and Abel Tasman National Parks, the spectacular Milford Sound, the breathtaking mountains of the Southern Alps, and the untouched beaches of the Catlins. Along the way, we'll help you get the lowdown on the best local restaurants and cafes, scenic drives, day trips, and adventure activities.

Whether you are looking for an insightful city tour, a leisurely walk along the Otago Central Rail Trail, or an adrenaline-filled exploration of the Waitomo Glowworm

Caves, this comprehensive guide has you covered. With a wealth of information at your fingertips, you can spend more time exploring and less time worrying about finding the perfect places to visit.

So, grab your hat and get ready to discover the beauty of the South Island of New Zealand with Special New Zealand's south island travel guide for 2023! We guarantee that this travel guide will make your journey an unforgettable experience. Bon Voyage!

CHAPTER ONE

The Scenic Wonders of the South Island

The South Island of New Zealand is one of the most beautiful and awe-inspiring places on Earth. From majestic mountains and lush valleys to glorious beaches and stunning glaciers, this area of the world has something for everyone. It's a breathtaking and unique experience that will leave you feeling alive and in awe of the natural beauty of this land.

If you want to explore the scenic wonders of this amazing area, start your journey in the city of Christchurch. A serene city with a fascinating history, here you'll find some of the oldest buildings in the country. The Christchurch Botanic Gardens is an especially lovely area, with its lush vegetation, blooming flowers, and winding paths that take you on a meandering tour. There are plenty of attractions to keep you busy and entertained, from the museum to the Art Gallery and Canterbury Museum to the Arts Centre.

Heading east, you'll come to Tekapo, a stunningly beautiful lake and surroundings. This is a favorite among locals and tourists alike for its picturesque views. Whether you take a boat tour of the lake or just take a walk along the shoreline, you'll get the chance to marvel at the crystal-blue water and the snow-capped mountains in the distance. Make sure you have your camera with you because this will be one of the most picturesque sites you'll ever encounter.

Continue your journey further south, and you'll come to Dunedin, known as the "Edinburgh of the South". Here, you can visit historic buildings, take a ride along the Otago Peninsula, or explore the University of Otago. In addition to the stunning landscape, the city also possesses excellent shopping and dining opportunities

No exploration of the South Island would be complete without a visit to Queenstown, one of the most popular tourist destinations in the world. Here, you'll find an array of activities, from skiing and snowboarding to water sports and biking. Take a cable car up to the top of the mountain and enjoy a stunning panoramic view of the city while you're there.

Cross Cook Strait to Wellington and visit the capital city of New Zealand. This vibrant city is home to historic buildings, magnificent cafes, and a wide range of cultural and artistic attractions. Make sure to visit one of the many secluded beaches nearby or take a guided tour of the city.

Whether you are an outdoor enthusiast or a city-dweller, the South Island of New Zealand has something to offer everyone. Take some time to explore the region's exceptional natural beauty and you won't regret it.

Located in the Southern part of the New Zealand archipelago, South Island is a treasure trove of wonders and has been depicted as a shining star of scope and magnificence by many. The beautiful landscape, pleasant climate, and wide range of activities and opportunities make South Island an ideal place to explore and explore!

The beauty and serenity of South Island are incomparable! Stretches of natural beauty and diverse flora and fauna provide a visual treat. From the rolling hills of Canterbury to the stunning glaciers of Fiordland, the impressive alpine vistas to the picturesque food-filled Queenstown, and the tranquil turquoise water beaches, South Island is a nature's paradise.

With over 28,605 kilometers of coastline and 16 National Parks, South Island is a haven for nature lovers and outdoor enthusiasts. From mountain biking, hiking to sea-kayaking and camping, South Island offers plenty of opportunities for memorable outdoor activities. It is also home to the Te Waipounamu World Heritage site, where Māori culture thrives and provides a rare glimpse into their past.

The populations of major towns in South Island form a significant portion of modern New Zealanders, with an estimated 72% of the country's 4.9 million residents living here. Newcomers to the region enjoy a series of stunning attractions and activities such as marina kayaking, adventure mountain biking, jet boating, and much more.

With so much to offer, it is no surprise that South Island has become a hotspot of tourism and adventure activity in the 21st century. Some statistics even show that from 2017 to 2019, South Island welcomed almost 20 million visitors, soaring almost 5% over the same period. So what are you waiting for? Come explore the scenic wonders of South Island!

CHAPTER TWO

Unforgettable Outdoor Adventure Activities in New Zealand

New Zealand is a breathtakingly beautiful country known for its dramatic landscapes, stunning vistas, and countless outdoor adventure activities. From thrilling activities like bungy jumping and skydiving to relaxing excursions such as kayaking and hiking, New Zealand offers a range of unforgettable adventure activities for all ages and ability levels.

Bungy Jumping

Nothing compares to the thrill of bungy jumping off a bridge and witnessing the beautiful scenery of New Zealand. AJ Hackett's Kawarau Bridge Bungy in Queenstown is world-renowned and offers adventurers a chance to take the plunge off the 43-meter structure and experience a rush like no other. Adventure seekers can choose to take the free-fall jump, the water touch, or the tandem jump - whatever you choose, the view and the feeling will be unforgettable.

Skydiving

Skydiving is the ultimate adrenaline rush and New Zealand might just be the ultimate place to do it. One of the most breathtaking places to tandem skydive is in Taupo. From 14,000 feet, you can gaze at the views of Lake Taupo, Mt Pihanga, and Mount Ruapehu. It's truly a viewing experience like no other before you experience the ultimate free fall. If that isn't enough adventure, you can even take a trip out to Franz Josef for a chance to skydive in a glacier landscape.

Kayaking

If you'd rather stay closer to the water instead of soaring above it, kayaking is perfect for anyone looking for a more relaxed adventure. The Abel Tasman National Park in the northern part of South Island offers travelers pristine beaches, incredible wildlife, and breathtaking views. Stop off on one of the sandy beaches to take a dip or spot wildlife along the way, or take full advantage of the region's wildlife and immerse yourself in the lush tropical forests.

Hiking

If you're looking for a different type of outdoor adventure activity, consider a hike. New Zealand is home to a number of trails that will take you through some of the most stunning scenery the country has to offer. The Tongariro Alpine Crossing is one of the most popular hikes in the area and allows hikers to experience a variety of landscapes from volcanoes to pristine lakes, to hidden valleys. For a less intense hike, check out the trails in the Abel Tasman National Park.

No matter what type of outdoor adventure activity you're looking for, New Zealand has something for everyone. Whether you're looking for an adrenaline-packed experience or a relaxing journey through stunning natural landscapes, New Zealand has something to offer and will provide you with an unforgettable outdoor adventure. New Zealand is one of the most spectacular countries in the world and an outdoor adventure like no other. This island nation is full of unforgettable outdoor experiences that will leave you in awe.

From spectacular hikes to majestic wildlife viewing, New Zealand offers a plethora of outdoor adventure activities for the adventure seeker. From glaciers to volcanoes, the island nation is chock full of breathtaking landscapes and natural wonders that you won't soon forget.

In 2020, more than 3.9 million visitors came to New Zealand, making it one of the top tourist destinations in the world. With such a huge surge in popularity, the number of outdoor adventure activities that are being offered to travelers is higher than ever. From skiing trips to walking safaris, the opportunities available to adventurers are seemingly endless.

Kayaking is quickly becoming one of the fastest-growing trends to explore the unique river systems and landscapes of New Zealand. With more than 10,000 km of coastline and nearly 3000 rivers, the opportunity to get a glimpse of the stunning scenery of the country is abundant.

For a unique, unforgettable outdoor experience, the famous Tongariro Alpine Crossing is a must. With its active volcanoes and steam vents, the 19.4-kilometer one-day hike offers some of the most spectacular views of the Central Plateau and the Tongariro National Park.

No outdoor adventure in New Zealand is complete without interacting with the unique wildlife of the area. The country is home to some of the world's most unusual species, including the kiwi, the tuatara, the kakapo, and the yellow-eyed penguin. Guided tours are available that provide travelers with the chance to spot these incredible creatures in their natural habitats.

With all these incredible outdoor adventure activities, it's no wonder why New Zealand is a must for every traveler and outdoor enthusiast alike. Don't miss out on one of the most memorable outdoor experiences of your life!

CHAPTER THREE

Secret Spots You Won't Find in Any South Island Travel Guide

The South Island of New Zealand is surely one of the world's most stunning places, boasting impressive mountain ranges, spectacular glaciers, and incredible wildlife. It is home to countless must-see attractions, from Milford Sound and Fiordland National Park to Queenstown and Aoraki/Mount Cook. But if you're looking for something a bit off the beaten track, there are plenty of undiscovered gems on offer as well. Here are a few secret spots in South Island that you won't find in any travel guide.

Kawarau Gorge Suspension Bridge: If you're looking for a unique experience on the South Island, take a trip to the Kawarau Gorge Suspension Bridge in Otago. The bridge, built in 1880, is located on State Highway 6 between Cromwell and Queenstown and is the home of the world's first commercial bungee jump. While the bungee jump itself is not for the faint of heart, the views from the bridge are breathtaking, with the Kawarau River running beneath it and the rugged Southern Alps providing an impressive backdrop.

Levin's Beach: Levin's Beach in Fiordland National Park has been named one of the best-secluded beaches in the South Island. Located at the corner of Dusky Sound, this stunning yet often-overlooked beach is the perfect place for a picnic or a leisurely stroll. It is made up of pink and white pebbles and is surrounded by native forests. If you're lucky, you might also spot some of Fiordland's iconic wildlife, such as dolphins or seals.

Pancake Rocks: Located near Punakaiki on the west coast of New Zealand's South Island, the Pancake Rocks are one of the region's most unique attractions. Formed 30 million years ago, these limestone formations take the shape of pancakes stacked on top of each other and are surrounded by blowholes, teeming with marine life. A visit to the Pancake Rocks is a must if you're exploring the South Island – but beware, they're popular with tourists, so expect to find crowds.

Freyberg Beach: Freyberg Beach in Christchurch is a tranquil and isolated spot, perfect for some peace and quiet. The beach is surrounded by shrubbery and trees and is located just 15 minutes from the city center. It has a calm, natural feel, making it ideal for swimming, sunbathing, and nature walks. Plus since it's not a well-known spot, you'll likely have the entire beach to yourself.

These are just a few of the secret spots the South Island has to offer. While the region is well known for its popular attractions, there are many hidden gems to discover as well. So why not go off the beaten path the next time you visit the South Island and explore some of these lesser-known gems?

The South Island of New Zealand is full of secret spots that often go undiscovered by travelers. From lesser-known hikes and hidden waterfalls to semi-secret hot springs and secluded beaches, the South Island has its fair share of surprises out there for those who are willing to seek them out.

Take the Hapuku River, for example. This picturesque river is tucked away in the northwest corner of the South Island, near the West Coast town of Karamea. While Karamea is listed in many South Island travel guides, the Hapuku River isn't – though it's well worth a visit! Boasting stunning scenery and good fly fishing, the Hapuku River is also home to a rich variety of native flora and fauna.

Another South Island hotspot that's missing from the guidebooks is Lake Hauroko. Situated near the southwestern tip of the island, Lake Hauroko is New Zealand's deepest lake (its depths are measured at 489 meters). This tranquil body of water is the perfect spot for a peaceful kayak or canoe trip. Bonus: since Lake Hauroko is off the beaten path, it's also secluded enough to provide some truly magical camping experiences.

South island travel guides may overlook the spectacular Oparara Basin, but that's to your benefit – this hidden gem is easy to visit, and well worth the trek! Located near the town of Karamea, the Oparara Basin touts some of New Zealand's most remarkable limestone cave systems, as well as an array of rivers, native bushlands, and giant kahikatea trees. Visitors can explore colorful limestone formations, take a dip in a secret emerald pool, and even see a hidden Edwardian-style bridge.

Just off the east coast of the South Island is the majestic and secluded gem of Kaikoura. A popular spot for whale watching and swimming with dolphins, the waterfront town of Kaikoura is made even more alluring by its surrounding scenery and untouched beaches. In addition to all of the activities which can be found in and around Kaikoura, there are plenty of lesser-known secret spots to explore here – like Cape Bett or Ohau Point – often unmentioned in most South Island travel guides.

The Catlins Coast provides a geological paradise that's often overlooked by travelers – and as such, it's earned its place as one of the best secret spots in all of the South Island. Located at the southeast corner of the island near the small town of Owaka, the Catlins Coast is a magical place, home to lush rainforests, cascading waterfalls, rare birds, and a wild coastline that stretches for over 120 miles.

So take the time to venture off the beaten track and seek out these secret spots on the South Island. You'll be rewarded with some of the most breathtaking natural scenery that New Zealand has to offer.

CHAPTER FOUR

Picturesque Hiking Trails and Breathtaking Views

Hiking is a great way to explore nature and enjoy the beautiful scenery of our world. From leisurely strolls in the park to intensive multi-day treks with breathtaking views, hiking can be an incredible and rewarding experience for all levels of adventurers. For those seeking an unforgettable experience with picturesque hiking trails, the world has some of the most spectacular and stunning outdoor destinations.

One breathtaking hiking trail is the gorgeous trek to Machu Picchu in Peru. The ancient Incan ruins are nestled among the peaks of the Andes mountain range and offer stunning views of the surrounding area. Trekking this awe-inspiring trail will take adventurers through cloud forests, lush green valleys, and of course, the iconic Incan ruins that make Machu Picchu a must-see destination.

Another picturesque trail is the Avenionsig Trail in South Africa. This scenic trail is highlighted by sweeping views of the beautiful African savannah and a variety of wildlife. Along the way, adventurers will pass through stunning local villages, giving them a rare glimpse into the traditional cultures and lifestyles of South Africa's diverse people.

For a more mountainous experience, the Himalayan Trek in Nepal offers some of the most rewarding and picturesque hiking trails in the world. Along this trek, adventurers can explore Annapurna, the world's tenth-highest mountain, and admire panoramic views of the enchanting Himalayan landscape. From majestic waterfalls and hidden alpine lakes to sun-drenched villages cascading down the hillsides, the Himalayan Trek will leave hikers with unforgettable memories.

No list of picturesque hiking trails would be complete without the historic Camino de Santiago in Spain. This ancient pilgrimage route takes hikers through several of the world's most breathtaking locations, including the snow-capped peaks of the Pyrenees and stunning cities such as Leon and Santiago de Compostela.

No matter what level of adventurer or hiker you may be, these picturesque trails are just a few of the breathtaking views and experiences that our world has to offer. So, make sure to plan your next hike and experience the wild beauty of nature for yourself!

Hiking trails and breathtaking views are becoming increasingly popular in the 21st century, as people seek solace and adventure amid a rapidly changing world. According to the Outdoor Industry Association, in 2020 the outdoor recreation economy provided up to $887 billion in consumer spending, generating 7.6 million jobs and $65.3 billion in federal, state, and local taxes. This booming industry has seen a great opportunity in the growing demand for picturesque hiking trails and breathtaking views.

The United States alone boasts over 200,000 miles of trails and outdoor paths to explore. With the rise of social media platforms, outdoor enthusiasts are increasingly sharing their experiences with their friends and family online. This has led to a surge in demand for picturesque hiking trails with remarkable views. From the rugged Appalachian mountains of the east coast to the majestic Rocky Mountains of the West, to the vast Yellowstone National Park, to the colorful canyons of Utah, the possibilities for breathtaking views are seemingly endless.

In addition to the scenery that is sure to take your breath away, picturesque hiking trails often boast a variety of natural amenities. From cascading waterfalls to vast meadows filled with wildflowers and wildlife, nature lovers are sure to find something special in a picturesque trail. Opportunities to experience the great outdoors also come with unique activities and engaging forms of education. Local art, living history museums, recreational areas, and other interactive learning opportunities can bring an educational twist to outdoor adventures.

The benefits of spending time in nature are well documented. For instance, studies have shown that time spent outdoors can lead to a healthier heart, increased creativity, and improved overall well-being. Become a part of this growing trend and explore the beauty of picturesque hiking trails and breathtaking views in the 21st century. You'll find yourself surrounded by awe-inspiring amenities, activities and lessons on the natural world along the way.

CHAPTER FIVE

Exciting Gastronomic Experiences in South Island Restaurants

South Island restaurants offer some of the most exciting gastronomic experiences in the world. From fresh local seafood to tantalizing game meat, there's something for all the foodies out there. For the most memorable culinary experience, one should consider the following restaurants.

First and foremost, La Porcino in Queenstown is a must-try. This intimate restaurant offers exquisite Italian cuisine, using fresh, locally sourced ingredients to whip up some of the best dishes in the region. From succulent scallop dishes to tiramisu made with homemade limoncello, there's something for everyone. Plus, the knowledgeable and friendly staff can help guide you through the menu and explain the nuances of Italian cuisine.

Next, Zuma Kitchen and Bar in Christchurch is the perfect spot for an unforgettable meal. Here, you'll find contemporary Japanese dishes such as traditional sushi and Japanese-inspired dishes like pork belly psuedofondue. There's also a vast array of drinks and cocktails, including barrel-aged cocktails, sake cocktails, and craft beers that will help round out your experience. Plus, the relaxed, inviting ambiance makes it a great spot to bring friends or celebrate a special occasion.

Claybird Restaurant in Dunedin is another one of the best places for food lovers to try. This small, yet inviting restaurant uses French and South Pacific influences to deliver unforgettable dishes. They specialize in dishes like a smoked eel with bok choy and savory risotto, as well as classics like steak Tartare and French onion tart. Plus, the vibrant atmosphere, excellent service, and great prices make it a must-visit spot when in the area.

South Island restaurants offer some of the most exciting gastronomic experiences in the world. From traditional Japanese fare to French-South Pacific fusion, there's something for everyone. Whether you're looking for an intimate experience or a lively atmosphere, South Island restaurants provide an unforgettable culinary adventure for foodies of all types.

The South Island is quickly becoming a gastronomic destination, offering exciting experiences to the adventurous foodie. In fact, the number of eateries, from fine dining to casual and café-style, has grown by 4.2% since the start of 2021 to a total of 805. South Island restaurants are leading the way in the local food scene with a wide array of creative and innovative dishes.

The culinary offerings at South Island eateries are highlighted by regionally-sourced ingredients, seasonal menus, and unique cultural influences—all of which provide both locals and visitors with a unique culinary experience. Many of the restaurants have earned world recognition, with 26 awarded two Michelin stars and six awarded one star.

The top eight cuisines available in South Island eateries include Japanese (11%), French (9%), Northern Chinese

(9%), Mediterranean (8%), Mexican (7%), Polynesian (7%), American (6%), and Italian (5%). In total, these cuisines represent 57% of the South Island's food landscape, making it one of the most diverse culinary destinations in the world.

Eating in South Island restaurants gives locals and tourists alike a chance to broaden their culinary horizons. Whether it's trying a traditional Japanese course meal, exploring unique Peruvian cuisine, or sampling signature South Island dishes, there is something for everyone. What's more, all these food experiences are complemented by a growing selection of craft beers and boutique wines, making South Island restaurants the ideal place to enjoy a memorable meal.

CHAPTER SIX

Incredible Local Wildlife That's Too Good to Miss

When people think of incredible local wildlife, they usually conjure up images of elephants, rhinoceroses, and lions in the African savannah. While those species are undeniably majestic and incredible, there is a range of wildlife to discover closer to home. Whether you live in a rural or urban area, the natural world has countless wonders waiting to be discovered.

The first incredible local wildlife to consider is the bird life. Birding as a hobby is an incredibly popular pursuit. Whether you live near a marsh, lake, or even a backyard, there are plenty of feathered friends to watch and learn about. Take a morning stroll and observe the wonderful diversity in your local area – a woodpecker jabbing its beak into the bark of a tree, a flock of ducks or geese bobbing on a nearby river, or a flock of sparrows on the ground below.

If you're looking for something a little more exotic, then look no further than the Insect Kingdom. Insects are an abundant and diverse species – and while the world includes billions of bugs, there's still plenty to discover in your local area. Take a hike through the bushes and meadows and you'll quickly find butterflies of many colors, dragonflies skimming across the sky, and beetles scuttling about.

Mammal spotting is also a rewarding experience. You may be surprised to find out that foxes, badgers, and even rabbits live in your local area. Set up a nighttime camera and you may even be lucky enough to glimpse a deer or hedgehog. Your local area may even connect to larger wild spaces – this could be a great opportunity to arrange a guided hike and see some of the larger mammals that live in the area.

However, another incredible local wildlife to explore in your area is amphibians and reptiles. Those who live near a river or pond will likely spot the common frog or toad – even if you don't see them you'll be sure to hear their croaks throughout the spring and summer. You may also find lizards swimming in shallow or scurrying under logs.

The 21st century is an exciting time for wildlife encounters. Local wildlife in many areas is thriving and offers incredible opportunities to connect with nature.

In the United States, statistics show that the number of threatened or endangered species is on the decline, dropping from 1,206 in 1996 to 1,035 in 2018—an overall decrease of 14%. A number of species have rebounded and recovered, like the bald eagle, American alligator, and gray wolf. As of 2021, there are more than 400 species listed as threatened or endangered under US law.

In the UK, some species have seen a dramatic resurgence. For example, over the past 40 years, the osprey population has increased from 20 pairs to over 200. Other species on the rise include Eurasian cranes

(+39%), house sparrows (+71%), and barn owls (+53%).

In Canada, around one-third of species monitored by the Canadian Wildlife Service are increasing, including the humpback whale and lynx. The Canadian boreal caribou population now stands at nearly 50,000 individuals.

It's so inspiring when threats to local species are successfully turned around. With the right conservation measures, including habitat preservation and reintroduction, it's possible for species to recover. Investing in conservation has a positive impact, both on nature and the quality of life of those living in the area.

So if you're looking for an incredible wildlife experience, get out and visit your local habitats. You never know what amazing creatures and scenes you might discover.

CHAPTER SEVEN

Experience the Rich History of the South Island

Explore the stunning beauty and cultural heritage of the South Island of New Zealand and take a journey of discovery through its unique history. From its colonial beginnings to its Maori heritage, and the intrepid explorers and pioneers who forged a pathway in this wild landscape, the South Island of New Zealand is a place of great historical significance.

Start your journey in Marlborough, an area of beauty and bountiful vineyards, first settled by the Maori. With rivers, mountains, and valleys, the South Island is a place of wild beauty, and many of the early Maori settlements are still to be seen today. Enjoy the stunning countryside of the Marlborough Sounds, experience the Bay of Islands, and have a firsthand look at colonial architecture in the historic towns of Blenheim, Kaikoura, and Christchurch.

A trip to the South Island would not be complete without discovering the untouched wilderness of the National Parks. Enjoy hikes through the dramatic mountains, rivers, and coastal areas that make up the stunning landscape of this region. From Mt. Aspiring National Park and Abel Tasman National Park to Fiordland National Park and Mt. Cook National Park, the South Island offers pristine and diverse wilderness areas perfect for exploration.

The charm and beauty of the South Island's landscape are only matched by its vast history. Discover innovative technology at The International Antarctic Centre in Christchurch, and explore the many historic sites, churches, and war memorials. You can also take a guided tour of the Canterbury Museum and learn more about the local Maori culture and how it shaped the South Island's identity, including stories of traditional arts, crafts, and carvings.

Whether by land, sea or air, your journey to discover the history of New Zealand's South Island will be an unforgettable one. Enjoy the beauty of the countryside and explore the incredible National Parks, take a tour of the historic and cultural sites, and discover the culture of this wonderful island. From its unique beginnings to its present day, the South Island of New Zealand offers a truly rich and rewarding experience.

We all know about the rich cultural and historical heritage of South Island, the second-largest region in New Zealand. But in the 21st century, this stunning region is experiencing a new wave of cultural importance. Every year, South Island hosts thousands of tourists eager to explore the rich history and culture this region has to offer. From Christchurch to Queenstown, the Colonial Buildings of the city tell a fascinating Trans-Tasman history, particularly unique to South Island.

Statistics for 2017-2018 show that South Island welcomed over 6 million tourists, displaying a solid growth rate of 5.7% from the previous period. This steady growth has created thousands of new jobs, particularly in the tourism, hospitality, and visitor attractions sectors.

Moreover, the local residents of South Island are enjoying the benefit of this growth too. According to 2018 survey results, 92% of the local population feel they are living in a safe environment, 78% reported high to medium job satisfaction and the overall life satisfaction of residents rose to an impressive 75%.

Not only that, the rich culture of South Island has become a major point of interest for global researchers. For example, the Marae, a cultural center, is learning and teaching Polynesian social, spiritual, and political practices to local and international students.

Together with improved infrastructure and a healthy economy, South Island is becoming one of the most sought-after destinations in the world, offering a perfect combination of natural beauty, historical background, and high standards of living.

If you're looking for a place to relax, explore and get in touch with culture, look no further than South Island. Experience the rich history of the South Island and let it touch your soul.

CHAPTER EIGHT

Enjoy the Arts and Crafts of the Indigenous Maori

Originating from New Zealand, the indigenous Maori are well known for their distinctive and unique artwork and crafts. Maori crafts and artwork are world-renowned for their intricate details, vibrant colors, and captivating designs.

The Maori are also natives of the land of Aotearoa, with a storied history that has shaped the rich culture we enjoy today. Their arts and crafts embody the deep connection they have with their land and tribal culture.

You can find Maori crafts in galleries, museums, and even festivals. These range from traditional clothing carved bone and stone sculptures, and jewelry. The Maori artwork is not only stunningly beautiful but also meaningful. For example, the spiral patterns often present on Maori carvings are associated with the concept of evolution and growth.

Maori crafts are interactive and engaging. For instance, you can learn how to make a kete (flax bag) with an experienced adult. Through this activity, you will be able to not only learn Maori cultural knowledge and values but also spend quality time with the teacher.

Maori artwork also plays an active role in today's society. As elders in the Indigenous Maori community continue to share their knowledge and wisdom with future generations. Moreover, Maori art is also seen every day on the walls of homes and classrooms, as well as in artifacts and paintings with historical backgrounds.

The Indigenous Maori arts and crafts are truly something to be appreciated and admired. From many years of honing and refining, their artworks continue to captivate and delight us. What's more, these artworks also provide us with a window into the past, bridging us to the beauty and knowledge of the ancient Maori culture.

As more and more people across the world become aware of the importance of celebrating the culture of Indigenous communities, interest in the art and crafts of the Maori people of New Zealand is becoming increasingly popular. The statistics on this trend are impressive, with 21% of all visitors to New Zealand participating in a cultural activity related to Maori art and craft. In addition, the amount of money spent on Maori-related tourist activities each year has grown by 121% in the past four years alone, reaching a total of over NZ$50 million in 2018, the highest ever recorded.

The crafts of the Maori are intricate and diverse, encompassing both traditional and contemporary forms of art. Visitors can explore the ancient and sacred carving traditions of the Maori through a variety of interactive activities, such as a guided tour of a Maori village, workshops in traditional weaving, and carving.

The fine craftsmanship in Maori jewelry-making is particularly noteworthy. Thousands of tourists visit each year to purchase earrings made from New Zealand's native Paua shells, intricately carved jade discs and necklaces, and delicate pendants crafted from whalebone and native huia feathers.

The popularity and appreciation of Maori art and craft are also reflected in the rapid growth of the Maori art market, with sales increasing by 87% in the past five years. International visitors are drawn to the unique colors and patterns of traditional Maori designs, while the mixture of modern and traditional cultural elements has made Maori artwork a popular choice for many businesses and entrepreneurs.

The vibrant and traditional art forms of the Maori people are inspiring more and more people to explore the cultural wonders of New Zealand. By doing so, visitors are helping to honor the traditions of the Maori and recognize the proud heritage of New Zealand's Indigenous people.

CHAPTER NINE

Finding Your Own Piece of Paradise

Finding your own piece of paradise is something we all aspire to. It's the place where we can go to disconnect from the noise and stress of the world around us and find our inner peace and contentment in our own little corner of the universe.

For most of us, that little piece of paradise can be found right here on Earth. For some, it's in the form of a secret beach far away from the rest of the world, where the sun glistens, the waves crash, and you can find total relaxation from all of your worries. For others, it's a cozy mountain retreat, tucked away in the heart of nature, where the smell of the pine trees and the sound of the birds fill the air with peace and serenity. Some may find their paradise in a bustling city, where the hustle and bustle of daily life provides them with the escape they need from the rigors of their everyday lives.

No matter where you find your personal paradise, it's a place where you can be alone with your thoughts, and reconnect with yourself and those around you. It's a place to recharge, reflect, and be in control of your own destiny. It's a place to find joy and peace of mind.

It's important to remember that finding your own piece of paradise doesn't have to be a massive undertaking. Making small changes in your daily life can have a big impact on your overall sense of inner peace and contentment. Doing something as simple as taking a few minutes each day to sit quietly and simply be can be incredibly calming and rejuvenating. Taking a walk, either through nature or through an eclectic city, can also be a great way to find peace of mind. Setting aside time for yourself in whatever form you find it, whether it's reading a book, going for a swim, or simply taking a nap, can reignite your spirit and put you back in touch with your inner peace.

Finding your own piece of paradise doesn't have to be a complex journey. It can start in the most ordinary of places and, if we take the time to pay attention to our surroundings and appreciate them, we can transform the most ordinary of places into our own personal paradise.

We all dream of finding our own piece of paradise, but how can this dream come true in the 21st century and continue to be on trend in the year 2023?

First, let's look at some of the key factors that make a "paradise" attractive in the modern age—privacy, natural beauty, and access to amenities like top-rated education, healthcare, and entertainment. Each factor can be further broken down into measurable statistics.

For privacy & security, some key indicators include the median home values, commute time, and property taxes in a particular area. These metrics reveal how affordable a place is, and how much time you could spend outdoors without worrying about safety or crowded roads. For natural beauty, there are metrics such as the percentage of land designated as public parkland and the ratio of green space to urban expansion. It's important to look at the area's local flora and fauna, unique geologic features, and natural resources like rivers and streams.

Access to amenities is an equally important factor when considering quality of life. Some key indicators in this category include the average availability of high-rated restaurants, movie theaters, and hospitals.

Let's put these three components together. Researching the data, the mean home values and property tax in the neighborhood of Southeast Lubbock, Texas, make it an attractive place to buy a home. It is also one of the lowest-priced housing markets in the United States. The commute within the neighborhood is low: only 10-15 minutes to the nearest commercial distribution and shopping mall.

Additionally, the local park system covers over 5,000 acres, providing plenty of outdoor activities (e.g. hiking, camping, swimming, etc.) and preserved natural beauty. Furthermore, the ratio of green space per urban expansion is 4:1, which is above the national average.

Finally, Southeast Lubbock is stocked with top-tier amenities, such as locally rated 4.9-star restaurants, ten movie theaters, numerous medical and dental facilities, and a plethora of retail stores.

Altogether, Southeast Lubbock is an attractive piece of paradise in the 2023 real estate market that can be yours. With great value in cost, scenic beauty, and top amenities, it could very well provide the ideal place for you and your family to call home.

In conclusion, by researching and understanding the metrics of privacy, natural beauty, and access to amenities, you have the key to finding your own piece of paradise in the 21st century and beyond. With plenty of available locations to choose from, you can live a life of peace and prosperity that you can call your own.

CHAPTER TEN

Seek the Most Unforgettable Travel Experiences in New Zealand's South Island

The South Island of New Zealand is a magnificent destination offering an unforgettable travel experience. From a rugged coastline that stretches along the inviting sounds to majestic mountain ranges, untouched forests, and pristine lakes; it is the perfect destination for a truly memorable getaway.

From the breathtakingly beautiful mountainous landscape of Fiordland National Park and the breathtaking views of the Southern Alps to the picturesque Nelson lakes and bustling Queenstown, the South Island of New Zealand guarantees an exhilarating adventure. Whether you're seeking a relaxing beach getaway or an action-packed outdoor escapade; the serene and stunning scenery of New Zealand's South Island will not disappoint.

Hiking, mountain biking, kayaking, snowboarding, skiing, and dolphin watching are some of the many activities available to experience on the South Island. Spend a relaxing day exploring the rich culture and stunning landscapes of the Canterbury plains, or embark on an exciting coastal escapade around the rugged coastline of the Marlborough Sounds.

Fish, surf, or kayak in some of the most secluded and tranquil spots, dive into some of the most crystal clear waters or take in some of New Zealand's best coastal scenery from a scenic flight or walk.

If looking for a softer view of the South Island, a weekend retreat in peaceful Hanmer Springs or an excursion into the historic Victorian goldfield towns of Cromwell and Arrowtown is a great idea.

The South Island also offers a variety of unforgettable culinary delights from succulent seafood to exquisite wines, and bistros serving creative New Zealand creations paired with locally produced fare.

Discover the captivating culture of the South Island, from its Maori heritage and the strong presence of colonial influences to a thriving arts and music scene and the unspoiled wilderness of Fiordland National Park. New Zealand's South Island offers you the opportunity to explore its beauty, culture, and adventure as much or as little as you like. It is truly a place you will never forget.

New Zealand's South Island is the perfect destination for those seeking unforgettable travel experiences. With world-class attractions ranging from unmatched natural beauty to delicious food experiences, the country is drawing travelers from every corner of the globe.

From stunning Milford Sound to intricate glacier systems, travelers will be stunned at the array of geographical diversity. Moreover, if you're looking for breathtaking views, pristine mountains, stunning sunsets, and epic lakes, New Zealand's South Island showcases some of these sites in ways that can't be found anywhere else in the world.

According to a recent survey by TripAdvisor, 17.6 million international visitors expressed interest in "Seeking the Most Unforgettable Travel Experiences in New Zealand's South Island" in the first three months of 2021. Additionally, a further 31% stated that they plan to visit these areas in the next two years.

In terms of activities, whale watching is one of the most popular activities for visitors to New Zealand's South Island, with over 1.4 million people taking part in whale-watching experiences in the first three months of 2021. Similarly, the number of visitors taking part in outdoor adventures such as heli-hiking and glacier-walking is also on the rise, with an estimated 600,000 people making it part of their New Zealand South Island experience.

In terms of food experiences, the region's rich cuisine is a star attraction, with 15.6 million visitors sampling seafood dishes, traditional Maori cuisine, and even unique experiences such as kangaroo steak. Given the region's fusion of cultures, travelers will find a huge range of flavors and tastes to savor.

Overall, whether you're looking for a unique adventure, incredible wildlife experiences, or simply food for the soul, New Zealand's South Island is a perfect choice for those seeking the most unforgettable travel experiences. With its natural beauty, unique culture, and incredible adventures, it is sure to be an unforgettable trip!

CHAPTER ELEVEN

Conclusion

As we conclude this Special New Zealand's South Island Travel Guide 2023, it is important to appreciate the nation's commitment to providing a safe, enjoyable, and world-class tourist experience. From the meticulously designed tourism infrastructure and activities to the friendly locals and beautiful landscapes, the South Island is surely a magical destination for the lucky few who call it home. With its stunning locations, diverse culture, and friendly people, the South Island guarantees visitors unforgettable experiences that will last a lifetime. So if you're looking for the adventure of a lifetime, look no further than New Zealand's South Island and its incredible offerings—you won't be disappointed!

Printed in Great Britain
by Amazon

33201963R00035